# LOOK AND FIND®

DISNEP PRESENTS A PIXAR FILM

# THE INCREDIBLES

ILLUSTRATED BY ART MAWHINNEY
COVER INSET ILLUSTRATED BY THE DISNEY STORYBOOK ARTISTS

© DISNEY ENTERPRISES, INC./PIXAR ANIMATION STUDIOS
THE TERM OMNIDROID USED BY PERMISSION OF LUCASFILM LTD.

PUBLISHED BY
LOUIS WEBER, C.E.O.
PUBLICATIONS INTERNATIONAL, LTD.
7373 NORTH CICERO AVENUE
LINCOLNWOOD, ILLINOIS 60712

GROUND FLOOR, 59 GLOUCESTER PLACE
LONDON W1U 8JJ

WWW.PILBOOKS.COM

8 7 6 5 4 3 2 1

ISBN 1-4127-3223-9

IN THE GOLDEN AGE OF HEROES, THERE WAS PLENTY OF SAVING TO DO TO KEEP THE SUPERS BUSY. LOOK FOR THESE SUPERS AS THEY PROTECT MUNICIBERG FROM VILLAINOUS PLOTS AND MISFORTUNATE ACCIDENTS.

ELASTIGIRL

MR. INCREDIBLE

FROZONE

GAZERBEAM

THUNDERHEAD

DYNAGUY

STRATOGALE

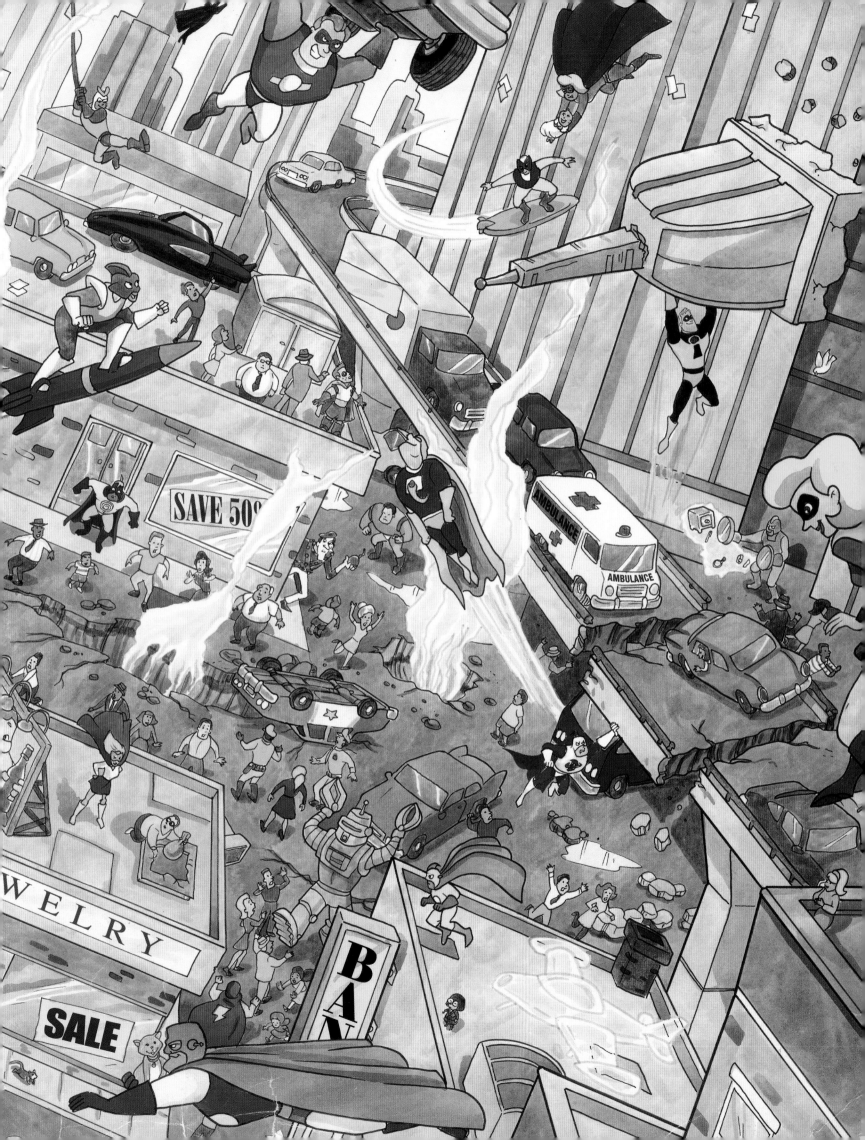

INSURICARE IS PROBABLY THE WORLD'S WORST INSURANCE COMPANY. WITH DRAB CUBICLES, A HEARTLESS BOSS, AND DISAPPOINTED CUSTOMERS, NO WONDER BOB MISSES DOING HERO WORK. TRUDGE THROUGH THE INSURICARE BUILDING TO FIND ALL OF THESE EVERYDAY OFFICE ITEMS.

DENIED STAMP

OFFICE MANUAL

INSURICARE COFFEEMUG

PAPER SHREDDER

RED TAPE

POSTER OF EMPLOYEE OF THE MONTH

CIRCULAR FILE

EVERY DAY CAN BE A CHALLENGE FOR SUPERS WHO ARE LIVING UNDERCOVER. IT'S DINNER WITH THE PARRS. THE DOORBELL IS RINGING, JACK-JACK IS MAKING A MESS, AND THE FOOD IS GETTING COLD. LOOK THROUGH THE DINING ROOM AND FIND THESE LEFTOVERS THAT THE PARRS ARE EATING.

LAST NIGHT'S MEATLOAF

FROZEN DE-LITE

SUNDAY PEPPERS

MEXI-CORN CARNE

BUSY-DAY CASSEROLE

CHEEZY ROLL-UP

CHERRIES JUBILEE

**M**R. INCREDIBLE HAS ARRIVED AT THE REMOTE ISLAND OF NOMANISAN IN ORDER TO BATTLE SYNDROME'S LEARNING ROBOT, THE OMNIDROID. FIND THESE OTHER NIFTY INVENTIONS AND GADGETS WHILE MR. INCREDIBLE TAKES CARE OF THIS HI-TECH ROBOT.

YOU'VE JUST ARRIVED AT EDNA MODE'S SUPER-CLASSIFIED, TOP-SECRET LABORATORY. SHE'S BUSY AT WORK, COMING UP WITH ALL KINDS OF NEW FABRICS AND THREADS TO BUILD SUPER SUITS THAT ARE INDESTRUCTIBLE AND FASHIONABLE. TRY TO FIND THESE DESIGNS OF NEW SUPER SUITS.

A MASK

A HOMING DEVICE CONTROL

BOOTS

BODY SUIT

A FULL SUIT

GLOVES

BELT

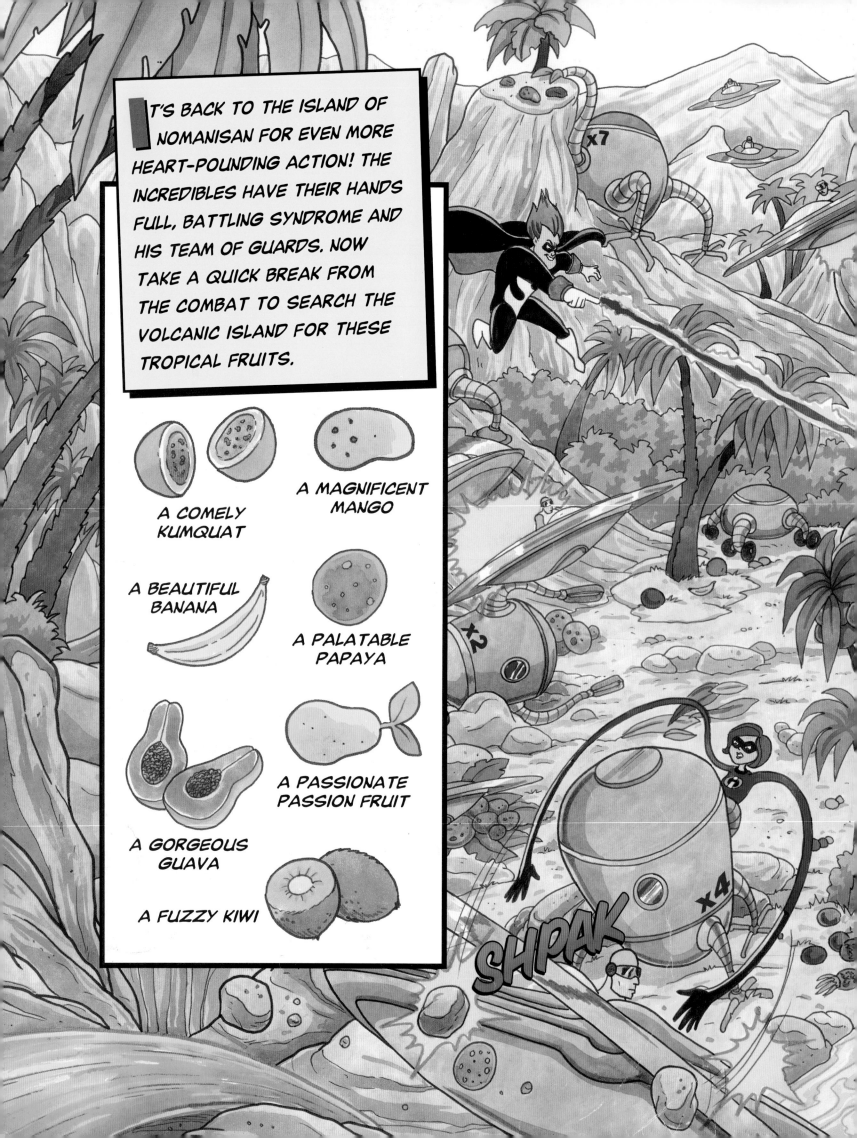

IT'S BACK TO THE ISLAND OF NOMANISAN FOR EVEN MORE HEART-POUNDING ACTION! THE INCREDIBLES HAVE THEIR HANDS FULL, BATTLING SYNDROME AND HIS TEAM OF GUARDS. NOW TAKE A QUICK BREAK FROM THE COMBAT TO SEARCH THE VOLCANIC ISLAND FOR THESE TROPICAL FRUITS.

A COMELY KUMQUAT

A MAGNIFICENT MANGO

A BEAUTIFUL BANANA

A PALATABLE PAPAYA

A GORGEOUS GUAVA

A PASSIONATE PASSION FRUIT

A FUZZY KIWI

**F**INALLY, A HAPPY ENDING! THE PARRS ARE BACK TO THEIR NORMAL LIVES, AS NORMAL AS CAN BE FOR AN UNDERCOVER SUPER FAMILY. DASH MAKES SURE TO COME IN A CLOSE SECOND AT THE SCHOOL TRACK MEET. SEARCH THE TRACK AND BLEACHERS TO FIND SOME OF DASH'S CLASSMATES.

HEAD BACK TO THE GOLDEN AGE OF HEROES TO FIND THESE ACTION VEHICLES:

- [ ] THE INCREDIBILE
- [ ] UPSIDE-DOWN POLICE CAR
- [ ] CITY AMBULANCE
- [ ] FIRE ENGINE
- [ ] STRETCH LIMO
- [ ] INVISIBLE JET

RE-ENTER INSURICARE AND FIND THESE BUSY OFFICE WORKERS:

- [ ] WINDOW WASHER
- [ ] COMPUTER GEEK
- [ ] JANITOR
- [ ] TYPEWRITER REPAIR PERSON
- [ ] WATER COOLER MAINTENANCE PERSON
- [ ] MAIL DELIVERY PERSON
- [ ] SECURITY OFFICER
- [ ] COPY CLERK

**ZAM!**

RETURN TO THE PARR DINING ROOM IN ORDER TO FIND ALL OF THESE FAMILY KEEPSAKES:

- [ ] HEIRLOOM POCKET WATCH
- [ ] DASH'S BRONZED BABY SHOES
- [ ] PHOTO OF THEIR HAWAIIAN VACATION
- [ ] SOUVENIR PLATE FROM THE CAPITAL
- [ ] VIOLET'S SILVER BABY CUP
- [ ] HELEN AND BOB'S WEDDING PORTRAIT
- [ ] MATCHING WEDDING GOBLETS

FLY BACK TO THE ISLAND OF NOMANISAN TO FIND EVEN MORE GADGETS:

SNEAK BACK INTO E'S LAB TO FIND THESE HI-TECH TOOLS:

- [ ] SONIC SCISSORS
- [ ] TAPE RECORDER
- [ ] TEK-LON PATTERN PROJECTOR
- [ ] MICRO SEWING MACHINE
- [ ] TEST PILOT IV
- [ ] VACUUMFORM